ISBN: 978-1-9996335-6-1

Also available by this author and illustrator:

Teal Zebra

https://tealzebra.square.site
Instagram @tealzebradesign

ENDANGERED ANIMALS

'Who am I?' Rhymes

Dedicated to my dad, Mike, for teaching
me about nature from a young age!

Written & Illustrated by Rachel Hudson

I will describe some
endangered animals to you,
can you guess what they are
if I give you a clue?

Who am I?

I am the largest animal to ever exist.
My blowhole shoots 9 metres of sea mist.

Overfishing is causing oceans to drain,
impacting the whole of my food chain.

I can swim 30mph with my powerful tail.
Who am I?...

I am a Blue Whale!

Who am I?

Across Africa and Asia, there are 8 different species.
In China I am eaten as one of their delicacies.

I do not have teeth but I love to eat ants.
I am the most trafficked animal, it is pretty pants!

Covered in scales, my tongue is long and thin.
Who am I?...

I am a Pangolin!

I am found in the Russian Far East snow.

I carry and hide my prey as I go.

Humans are burning my habitat
and poaching me, as I am a spotty cat.

There are so few of us, I am critically endangered.

Who am I?...

I am an Amur Leopard!

Who am I?

In rainy season I build nests in trees,
I am a herbivore who eats fruits and leaves.

Our future relies on conservation,
to prevent hunting and deforestation.

I am the most endangered ape in Africa.
Who am I?...

I am a Cross River Gorilla!

Who am I?

Expansion of palm-oil plantations,
is leading to deforestation.

I sometimes trample humans' crops,
looking for food, trying not to get shot.

A peaceful coexistence is what I want.
Who am I?...

I am a Sumatran Elephant!

Who am I?

Global warming is causing bleaching,
killing the coral reefs that I live in.

I eat sponges, which are toxic to others,
cleaning it from the reef that it covers.

I am sold for my beautiful tortoiseshell.
Who am I?...

I am a Hawksbill Sea Turtle!

Who am I?

Although you may think I am white,
I am actually black and reflect visible light!

I see the effects of global warming,
all around me ice caps are melting.

My blubber insulates me from the frosty air.
Who am I?...

I am a Polar Bear!

Who am I?

In Spanish, my name means 'little cow'.
I am on the brink of extinction right now.

My home is a world heritage site,
but sometimes there is illegal fishing at night.

I am a marine mammal in the Gulf of California.
Who am I?...

I am a Vaquita!

Who am I?

I live in Borneo, an island in Asia.
I have a broad face and orangey fur.

I swing from treetops and that is where I nest.
My name translates to 'man of the forest'.

I eat with my feet and use tools like a human.
Who am I?...

I am a Bornean Orangutan!

Who am I?

My roar can be heard from 2 miles away,
I can jump 10 metres to pounce on my prey!

Critically endangered, our numbers are declining,
my main threats are deforestation and poaching.

I have heavy black stripes and orange fur.
Who am I?...

I am a Sumatran Tiger!

Who am I?

My skin is grey and leathery,
my horns are traded like ivory.

Ox-pecker birds help keep me clean
and warn me when a predator is seen!

I am nature's unicorn without the rainbow.
Who am I?...

I am a Black Rhino!

These endangered species
are ever so rare,
let's all do our part
to show that we care!

Printed in Great Britain
by Amazon